MW00330932

Recognition for *Straight Talk your Way to Success* by Best-Selling Authors and International Speakers

"This book is as powerful as it is simple. And that's the point. The world truly needs more reminders of this kind of wisdom."

~ PATRICK LENCIONI; president, The Table Group; bestselling author, *The Five Dysfunctions of a Team and The Advantage*

"In this crisp and timely book, Dan Veitkus exposes the communication traps that stand in the way of even the smartest people. Figure out how to deliver Straight Talk, and watch your leadership, consulting or sales career take off. Because at the end of the day, making real connections is the secret to success."

~ TIM SANDERS, author of *Love is the Killer App: How To Win Business & Influence Friends* and former CSO at Yahoo!

"This book is a page turner — a beautiful blend of home spun wisdom, the most up to date research and compelling storytelling. I believe that leaders who embrace the principles in this book will indeed fast track their way to success and simultaneously create an empowering vibrant culture within their organization."

~ KEVIN KELLY, Internationally acclaimed leadership speaker and Best Selling Author

Global Praise from Business and Political Leaders for *Straight Talk your Way to Success...*

"*Straight Talk your Way to Success* will help every professional, no matter industry or dreams, achieve the best that is within you and maximize your potential through a simple but critical approach to achieve effective communication.

The Straight Talk Principles are masterful. I have not found a more effective approach to achieve success in how I communicate in politics, business, and family relations.

Straight Talk isn't just a great book about how to achieve effective communication and success. It describes the very essence of how Dan lives his life and how he approaches his passion for coaching the best out of others."

~ Senator Aaron Osmond, Salt Lake City, UT, U.S.A.

"Straight Talk offers practical wisdom for success in your life and career. It is a must-read for anyone, in any profession, both in the Eastern and Western world."

~ Walter Fang, SVP and CTO,
iSoftStone Group, Beijing, China

"Successful business leaders know that sustainable success is dependent upon smart and consistent execution, not smart talk. Dan outlines how to replace "smart talk" with "smart execution" through seven simple and compelling Straight Talk Principles."

~ Ken Muir, CEO, GWAVA, Montreal, Quebec, Canada

"From Dan Veitkus, one of the most inspirational and articulate leaders I have had the privilege to know, comes this powerful insight on leadership success and effectiveness.

In his clear and straightforward style Dan reveals the key secrets that turn managers into successful leaders, inspiring respect and admiration from their peers and colleagues.

Straight Talk will help you gain professional success and effectiveness and dramatically improve your productivity."

~ Dr. Mark Spiteri, Cambridge, U.K.

STRAIGHT TALK

TALK

YOUR WAY TO

SUCCESS

DAN VEITKUS

For information about this title or to order other books and/or electronic media, contact the author at: danveitkus.com

Library of Congress Control Number: 2014905730

ISBN:
978 099 14137 06 Hardcover
978 099 14137 13 eBook
978 099 14137 20 Paperback

Printed on recycled paper when possible

Cover and Interior design: 1106 Design, Phoenix, Arizona

To Grandma Adeline

*Master of Straight Talk
and Best Friend*

"Any fool can make things bigger, more complex, and more violent. It takes a touch of genius — and a lot of courage — to move in the opposite direction."

Albert Einstein

Contents

Introduction

"Direct and easy communication...
has become vital to the very survival
of a civilized humanity."

Walt Disney

TOO MUCH OF WHAT IS thrust upon us today as "communication" is simply inefficient and ineffective, and in many cases, incoherent and just plain noise. The truth is, we are living in the midst of a "Smart Talk" epidemic.

This is a book about a critical set of distinctions. It will expose the difference between spending time, energy, and intellectual firepower trying to *sound* smart and savvy — what I condemn as "Smart Talk" — and the more effective choice to *speak and operate deliberately* in order to avoid confusion, frustration, and wasted time, and therefore dramatically improve our productivity.

In *Good to Great*, author Jim Collins proclaimed, "Good is the enemy of great." This book will set another maxim for our time: "Smart Talking is the enemy of Smart Execution."

It's Time for Some Straight Talk

The whole point of Straight Talk is to *keep it real*. It's as simple and as difficult as returning to our original state of being authentic speakers and authentic listeners. This book exposes common Smart Talk Traps and offers seven Straight Talk Principles that will:

- ✦ Quickly help you become more productive, communicate more clearly, and expertly detect Smart Talk trash.
- ✦ Allow you to learn (or re-learn) the secrets to more productive conversations, communication, and relationships.
- ✦ Identify the distinction between *Straight Talk* that produces results and harmony and *Smart Talk* that brings only disappointment and ultimately, a crash-and-burn finale.

This book is for everyone, but if you're in the corporate and professional trenches, please take note! When Morgan Stanley recently analyzed the most successful public technology companies, they found three overwhelming attributes of all top performers: 1) a simple and focused mission, 2) an effective management team, and 3) a great culture. This book will help you understand that no person or organization can achieve these enduring characteristics without Straight Talk.

The Straight Talk Principles are inspired by the greatest wisdom of the past, colored with personal experience from the present, and organized for the benefit of our future. Some of the principles may not be new for you. But if you make them part of your "operating style," you'll achieve more positive outcomes as you communicate deliberately, honestly, and sincerely — the Straight Talk way.

The real insight is this: *You were there!* We were all born Straight Talkers. But when we "grew up," we strayed from being authentic. We swallowed the diet of Smart Talk jargon and breathed in the empty influences that pulled us further away from our Source and from our very nature as Straight Talkers! Think about any conversation you've had with a child and you'll recognize the difference between pure, unadulterated Straight Talk and the Smart Talk trash that permeates too much of our adult conversations.

> We were all born Straight Talkers. But when we "grew up," we swallowed the diet of Smart Talk jargon.

Confessions of a Smart Talker

Now, I'll admit it — there have been times when I've contributed to the Smart Talk epidemic that literally strips us of productivity, wastes our time and money, and renders all forward progress a chore. Yes, I've fallen for some of the common Smart Talk traps. I have no good excuse, nor do I attempt to justify these moments of failing the Straight Talk principles. I can only reflect on those moments and confirm without exception that they served no good purpose and they never produce the value generated from sticking to the Straight Talk path — with conviction. Should you be tempted to raise a self-righteous eyebrow or get out your bag of stones to throw, look in the mirror. Ask yourself, "Am I a Smart Talker, too?" You might be playing on the Smart Talk team or unwittingly falling into Smart Talk Traps that exist all around you.

Fear not! We've taken the first step toward renewing our well-being by identifying the problem. Now it's time to build a powerful recovery plan.

My Source of Wisdom: A Master Teacher

I was fortunate to have many positive Straight Talk influences in my life. And long before I entered a boardroom, I was blessed with the presence of a powerful teacher who gave me my first Straight Talk lessons.

4

Every master who takes on an apprentice applies the same formula: deliver the lesson, apply examples, demand practice of the skill, and then promote repetition. My personal teacher also demonstrated great patience while I learned and she provided swift reminders when I veered off track. This sage and confidante led by example and encouraged diligent practice.

My master teacher was and remains my paternal Grandmother, Adeline, who still lives an active life at the youthful age of 94. Grandma's personal story is rich with productive life lessons that could fill volumes. She has lived most of her life alone, as my grandfather passed away suddenly and far too young. She's tackled every one of life's little surprises with the wisdom of Socrates and the courage of the Trojans. Her four-foot-eleven-inch frame is a foundation of granite when it comes to preserving traditions, relationships, and life lessons that she believes are essential to living the good life. Wherever she lived, her little home was always recognized as a Zen garden for the minds, bodies, and souls of friends, family, and acquaintances who found rest, encouragement, and an obligatory bite to eat in Grandma's kitchen.

When I was growing up in the greater Chicagoland area, I'd ride my bike to her home as often as I could get away from school or work. It was through her lens on life that I first learned the distinction between Smart Talk and Straight Talk. Long before I logged millions of miles of business travel, Grandma was coaching me and guiding me toward the path of authentic living and a life full of great satisfaction, thanks to the practice of Straight Talk. The principles she taught me, reinforced by the experience I've had in practicing and promoting them around the world, make up the simple but effective gift of guidance I offer to you.

> She guided me toward the path of authentic living and a life full of great satisfaction, thanks to the practice of Straight Talk.

The Straight Talk Rewards

Why should we be concerned with the important distinction between Straight Talk and Smart Talk? Well, the reason is quite simple. When we eliminate Smart Talk trash from our lives and replace it with the promotion and practice of Straight Talk, we *will* be more successful, no matter what our profession or calling may be. "Success" can be a promotion, a target level of income, an annual dream holiday, harmony at home — *all of these and more*. However you chose to define success, this book will help you accelerate your progress toward those meaningful goals. If you find yourself stalled, this book will give you the tools, vocabulary, and confidence to cut the Smart Talk trash out of your life, and eliminate time-consuming distractions or wasted opportunities that keep you from defining and achieving the success you desire.

Are You Ready?

I've learned that our ability to deliver value is at the heart of any pursuit of happiness or success. And without question, we deliver greater value when our communication is clear, deliberate, and relevant. Now, I could further justify these timeless Straight Talk Principles with reams of data, but wouldn't

> We deliver greater value when our communication is clear, deliberate, and relevant.

that just add to the problem of quantity over quality? Instead, let's jump right toward our goal: *Living a life that's free of Smart Talk trash and rewarded with great success.*

Let's be *truly* smart and start Straight Talking — today.

CHAPTER 1

Ignorance Is Not Bliss

"What is necessary to change a person is to change his awareness of himself."

Abraham Maslow

GRANDMA ADELINE was the first person in my life to teach and reinforce the attributes of the first Straight Talk principle: *Be Aware and Stay Mindful.* Now what does this really mean? Is it as simple as: Be here now...enjoy the moment...listen for the music between the notes...stop to smell the flowers, the fresh-cut grass, or the burning leaves...listen to the birds chirping and the crickets calling? Yes, but there's a lot more to consider.

To avoid the trap of ignorance, we need to listen to others. Grandma Adeline is a world-class listener. From my earliest visits with her, I learned that the best teachers and wisest coaches are first and foremost great listeners. Grandma often says, "I haven't got a plane to catch!" — her way of inviting me to sit down and free my mind to explore life's dilemmas.

The Key: Listen and Ask Questions

A good listener asks thoughtful questions. A good listener asks questions to better understand not to interrogate. When Grandma does this, people find themselves saying, "Why didn't I think about 'it' that way?" Most important — and perhaps most profound — through sincere and generous listening, and questions without pre-judgment, Grandma taught me to genuinely seek to understand the context of a situation or conversation. Context is king when it comes to communication success and gaffes. Get it right and you'll raise the roof, move the student body, and inspire greater levels of commitment and engagement. Get it wrong and you may be ridiculed — or worse, you may invoke actions that are completely contrary to your intentions.

> Grandma taught me to genuinely seek to understand the context of a situation or conversation.

Grandma emphasized the importance of staying aware, and she stressed that ignorance is never *bliss,* but a poor soulmate of *negligence.* The ability to practice Straight Talk requires an acute awareness that trips an alarm if we slip into the Smart Talk Traps that will repeatedly create pain if we don't identify them and react to them immediately.

It Begins with Paying Attention to the Details

When I work with professionals, friends, or students, and whether my Straight Talk coaching sessions are formal or informal, I always start by observing and listening. I join people at meetings, shadow them on conference calls, or ask them to share written correspondence before they deliver it. The most valuable thing I can do as a Straight Talk coach is to listen carefully, *without judgment,* and take good notes. Then, it's easier to point out communication that is empty, superfluous, self-serving, and disingenuous, whether it's from the person I'm coaching or the people they're communicating with.

There are many good resources to improve your awareness and your ability to "read" gestures. If you want to dive deeper into this subject, try *How to Read a Person Like a Book* by Nierenberg and Calero.

It's important to "listen" to what you can't actually hear. Most of what is valued as profound communication is expressed without words. I'm sure you remember what it felt like to be a kid who made an error in judgment, seeing a parent approach with crossed arms and a frown! As adults, we know what it means when the person you're pouring your heart out to is checking email on an iPhone. We need to perfect our ability to read the signals that indicate that someone is reaching out to be heard, even silently.

"The Odd Couple"

When I was asked to join the coaching program at a large telecommunications firm early in my career, I was excited about formalizing my thoughts and approach to mentoring. I wanted to learn a disciplined approach to help develop other professionals. The program was really well organized, and the profiles and experience of all available "coaches" were open to any employee in the high-potential programs. In this way, people could knowledgeably select the person who would be a good match for their style and needs and offer the greatest value and support.

I'll never forget the afternoon when I heard a tap on my office door and I looked up to see John, a manager and 25-year veteran of the company. He asked if I would be his coach! He explained that he was determined to earn the director position that had eluded him for many years, and he thought I could help him adjust his approach.

Now, here's the surprise: John was 20 years my senior. But I had a secret advantage — Grandma Adeline — and I let her teaching point the way. John and I had worked together on various projects, so we knew each other on a business level. But I was keen to understand (and listen for) John's underlying interest in his professional pursuit, as well as why he chose me to be his coach. In our early sessions, we worked through specific steps he expected in his development and coaching program, along with his personal interests and the areas he wanted to improve.

> John was 20 years my senior but I had a secret advantage!

Although I was one of the youngest executive directors in the history of the company, John graciously expressed confidence in my leadership style and management approach, even though his tenure with the company exceeded my age. He also pointed out specific examples where — in his opinion — my presentations, communications, and style were more effective than most because I was deliberate, non-emotional, and willing to take accountability.

Now, John was asking for direct support in shifting his own approach to business and communication after decades of practicing a different style. He said, "You shoot straight, and people always know where they stand with you. I think this is why you're effective even if some of us have been here a lot longer."

> He needed someone who could help him craft his communications more deliberately and command greater accountability.

Without labeling my approach as Straight Talk, John understood and recognized its attributes. He was already *aware* — he knew that what he needed at that moment was someone who could help him craft his communications more deliberately, prepare more engaging presentations, and command greater accountability with customers, partners, and fellow employees.

In some respects, my part was made easy because I already knew the importance of awareness. All I had to do was remain authentic and focus on how to help John. It was also clear that John had the advantage of experience. This partnership helped *both* of us develop into better leaders for the firm. In our early days, some observers referred to us as the "odd couple," and those early impressions turned positive when people who had known John for years watched him refine his approach and make distinct changes. And he *did* earn that promotion. I learned a lot more about the inner workings of the firm. And I had more taps on the door asking for formal coaching relationships.

My experience with John helped me further develop my approach to coaching and mentoring and it strengthened my resolve to help others gain greater productivity at work and higher levels of personal achievement. It also reinforced the power of the Straight Talk Principles when they're practiced consistently and with purpose in a professional environment. Regardless of our background or experience, we can dramatically reshape our outlook and future by adjusting our approach when we see that we're falling for (and into) the Smart Talk Traps.

> We can dramatically reshape our outlook and future by adjusting our approach.

Straight Talk Principle #1

Listening without judgment is no simple affair! It requires discipline to turn off personal prejudices against communication styles, certain subject matter, and cultural norms so we can focus specifically on the effectiveness and real content of the communication.

The first Smart Talk Principle is *Be Aware and Stay Mindful.* Turning up your awareness is something you can practice on your own, but you may find great value in asking a trusted advisor, peer, or friend to support you. Brief them on this Straight Talk Principle and the benefits you're seeking. As you do, ask them to listen and provide feedback. They can help you turn up your awareness and they will also automatically improve their own awareness. Bit by bit, person to person, we'll reduce the epidemic of Smart Talk Traps!

The combination of learning and teaching at the same time is important and highly efficient. Thanks to Grandma's early guidance and encouragement, I've always been comfortable and eager to help others as a coach and mentor. She stressed two important points about learning and its relationship to teaching:

> First, when we learn something and choose to share it through teaching and coaching, we develop a *greater consciousness and richer context* for the lessons we ourselves

are trying to understand. We actually create the opportunity to practice what we're preaching.

The second point isn't original, but it's certainly universal: It does no good to keep our light (or moments of enlightenment) under a bushel basket! We should always *share our gifts* responsibly.

Now, with your awareness turned up, let's move on to the second principle.

How to Apply Straight Talk Principle #1:
Be Aware and Stay Mindful

The first step forward is *learning and practicing awareness*. This begins when we address our own contributions to the Smart Talk epidemic and staunchly refuse to surrender to its traps!

- Do some generous listening today. Listen to the intentions *behind* the words you hear. You may be surprised at the sheer volume of Smart Talk that's going on all around you!

- Practice "translating" non-verbal language. Watch from across a room, airport or restaurant and see if you can figure out what is being "spoken" without words.

- Do some non-workplace listening, too. When you're walking from your car to the office, take note of everything you hear, from the rumble of traffic to the wind in the trees. You'll tone up your listening muscles.

- When you're asked to listen, see if you can catch yourself wandering away mentally. Be gentle, but don't let that behavior continue!

"Let us not look back in anger or forward in fear, but around in awareness."

James Thurber

What the Research Reveals

In a 2012 blog post for *Harvard Business Review,* Anthony Tjan, CEO of the venture capital firm Cue Ball, focused on "how leaders become self-aware."

After researching his latest book, Tjan found that one quality that is evident in virtually every great entrepreneur, manager, and leader is self-awareness. Tjan says that self-awareness is essential and can't be considered "new era meditation" or soft science, and he concludes that <u>improving self-awareness about what motivates them is the best thing leaders can do to improve effectiveness</u>.

He says that self-awareness allows the leaders to "walk the tightrope of leadership: projecting conviction while remaining humble enough to be open to new ideas and opposing opinions." Tjan found that leaders' need for a certain amount of ego makes self-awareness even more essential. He suggests three ways to become more self-aware:

1. **Know yourself better** by using tests like Myers-Briggs and StrengthsFinder, which facilitates healthy and easy self-reflection, This will always lead to better self-awareness.

2. **Watch yourself and learn.** Tjan quotes Peter Drucker: "Whenever you make a decision, write

down what you expect will happen. Nine or 12 months later, compare the results with what you expected." This forces us to focus on both what we intended and the why behind our the decision, leading to progress in self-awareness and personal development.

3. **Be aware of others, too.** The best teams are rarely made up of similar types. If we're open-minded and objective, different types of people will help you further your self-awareness and deepen an appreciation for variety. This will allow you to see more clearly what you do well and what others do well.

For further reading: *Heart, Smarts, Guts, and Luck* by Anthony Tjan, Richard J. Harrington, and Tsun-Yan Hsieh (HBR Press).

CHAPTER 2

Artificial Complexity Stifles Productivity

"If you can't explain it simply, you don't understand it well enough."

Albert Einstein

WARNING! The words *complexity* and *productivity* may sound like boardroom talk, but they relate to many areas of life, regardless of your personal or professional calling. So even if you don't dwell in the Smart Talk-overdosed business world, please *don't be tempted to skip this chapter.*

Smart Talk noise is rampant in every walk of life — from politics to sports, from news coverage to newsmakers. But when you look at examples from the business world, you may better understand why many corporate warriors head home each evening looking like they've completed a mental marathon — tired, hungry, and spent.

I believe one of the reasons Smart Talk is now so pervasive is that it has successfully edged it's way into our lives over a sustained period of time. With the help of a few instigators, the proliferation steadily multiplies every day. However, if you know what to listen for, you can avoid the storm of lost productivity and frustration looming on the horizon at work or at home.

You Need Straight Talk in Daily Life

If you have the pleasure of the company of children in your home, you know firsthand when they are giving you a line that doesn't stack up! And whether they like it or not, they half-expect you to call them out and challenge the facts. But for some reason, as we grow older and contract the Smart Talk disease, we often forget our innate ability to form responses that challenge the nonsense with simple responses like *"Really?"*

Why do we do this? Well, there are many possible reasons. Is it because we want to fill our conference call time allotment, or cover an entire page? Do we need to quote the latest trendy expressions so we appear more intelligent? Are we secretly afraid that if we make our point in one simple statement, the world will think less of us? The reasons don't matter. What's important is we stop the insanity, one conversation at a time!

Consider this scenario: A farmer is responsible for the largest output of crops in a given area. After a devastating storm wipes out most of his planned harvest, he tells his family and shareholders, "I'm aggressively managing the decline in my planned production." Really? It sounds like he dropped from a spaceship into those crop circles or was sampling moonshine while driving his tractor. His family and shareholders would be left wondering, "What in tarnation is he talking about? Does he think we are stupid?" Yet, how many times have we heard similar expressions of nonsense from politicians, or co-workers?

> After a storm wipes out his harvest, a farmer says, "I'm aggressively managing the decline in my planned production."

If you are a farmer, a production manager or a chief executive, you can cut the Smart Talk trash and simply explain the situation, acknowledge your limitations, and just focus on what you can do and what may be possible. Replace the farmer in our story with your boss, your local politician or a fellow employee and far too often we find ourselves saying the same thing, "What is she talking about? Does she take me for stupid?"

You Need Straight Talk in Business

Most businesspeople have heard this line a million times: "Our priority is to grow the business." Wow, deep thoughts. How much do we pay these leaders for such profound insight? We certainly don't wake up in the morning looking to *kill* the business, do we? If we're going to fire up the troops, we need more than this! We need context, facts, and clear accountability by roles.

Just think how often a real message could have been reported in one or two clear, simple statements. Consider these two options, and note the obvious inefficiency and ample room for confusion generated by the Smart Talker:

✦ Smart Talker posting: All leaders and functional heads will convene to analyze and brainstorm various structural paths for our strategic initiatives and any key roadblocks we may encounter moving forward to maximize our aspirational goals and improve our productivity.

✦ Straight Talker posting: We will discuss our goals, both short and long term, what we believe is required to reach them, and what is necessary from every role.

And yet, statements like the former — along with an endless list of related mumbo-jumbo — are thrown around boardrooms and water coolers, at town hall meetings, and on conference calls every day. Press release quotes are littered with rambling statements that actually say *nothing* about the true intentions of a firm or its leaders. And when you've had to endure the Smart Talk spouting from the mouths of politicians around the world, I'm sure you've thought, "Cut the Smart Talk trash and tell the truth for once!"

> "One should aim not at being possible to understand, but at being impossible to misunderstand."
>
> *Quintilian*

Avoiding the Complex Doesn't Mean Eliminating Specifics

If you're going to practice Straight Talk instead of dwelling in the bottomless gutter of Smart Talk, you need to be *specific* about goals, what's possible, and the role of each person involved. *Specific* means citing *particulars*. To win the hearts, minds, and most important, the commitment of your family, business team, or community, you need to spell out the fine points and it helps to vividly describe the planned cause and effect. Here are some examples:

+ "If we set aside (specific amount) each month, we can afford one of these choices for our next family vacation. This is how we'll do that."

25

✦ "If we improve the operating income of the company by 5% this year, we can invest in three new product launches, hire 200 new staff members, and pay annual bonuses at 125%. Here's how we can make this happen."

✦ "If we improve the scores of our graduating students by x%, they'll have a 25% greater chance of getting financial aid for college, and this school will earn $X million in additional grants to develop the classroom of the future. Here's what will be required of each teacher and aide."

✦ "If we improve our pipeline by $100 million each quarter, given our historical conversion rates, we should improve annual sales by $30 million and be in a position to open that new office in Dubai. Let me show you how we can achieve that goal."

Straight Talk Principle #2

The second Straight Talk Principle is *Be Obvious and Keep It Simple*.

Let's begin with spoken communication and to be specific, "not email."

If you believe your choice of words and expressions have the potential to surprise your listeners as clever or well-educated prose, or you're expecting an audience to celebrate your genius, think again! Chances are you're playing to your ego and not the audience, and your real intentions and context will be lost. Befuddled audiences are never enthusiastic, and they surely won't stay engaged. Choose language, vocabulary and references that are relevant to your audience.

Why Email Isn't Always Best

Being Obvious and Keeping It Simple asks us to regain control and stop filling data networks with noise. If you absolutely want to improve results and the reception of your communication — regardless of the size, number, IQ, or disposition of your audience — *take the conversation off the electronic grid.*

Keeping it simple doesn't mean "make it as quick and easy on yourself as possible." In fact, some of today's most popular communication platforms — email, instant messaging, tweeting, and the like — pose the biggest threat to simplicity. Why? Because texting isn't talking. Email isn't dialogue. And tweeting is for birds.

Here's the issue laid bare: *Concentration* is missing from this kind of communication. These shortcuts feed and perpetuate thoughts that become keystrokes that become bits and bytes that become messages that become "fodder for the defense" as some celebrities are now learning the hard way. With no disrespect intended to those in the law profession, aren't we making it easy for both sides to dig up volumes of material that should have stayed buried in the cobwebs of the mind instead of twittering their way into the headlines and courtrooms?

Many Smart Talkers use email in particular to avoid in-person confrontation, a tactic also known as covering one's backside. If you'd put aside a little money every time you heard someone say, "I'm just covering my backside," you'd probably have your next holiday paid for. Those who go straight to the other party in question almost always report a more productive conversation and better outcome than using a string of emails or texts. One of the goals of Straight Talk is saving time, and there's no better way to avoid spending endless days on the same topic, debate, or question than by calling or visiting someone directly.

> Sending email is like loading the dishwasher for one plate. Yes, the final outcome is a clean dish, but do you really want to waste 45 minutes, poison the environment further, and consume precious water sources for just one plate? So it goes with email. Rarely does one message suffice. You wait and then respond, and you endure a cycle or two. And sometimes you still end up with a dirty dish and a phone call required.

Why Face-to-Face or Voice-to-Voice is Better Than Text

If the Smart Talk addiction of inserting every media and business school buzzword into a simple communication takes the prize for "biggest loser," then hiding behind a keyboard gets the Academy Award for "best supporting crutch." It's easy for our true intentions to get lost in the bang-click-send algorithms that produce millions of email and instant messages — most of which go unread, unappreciated, or misunderstood.

When you text instead of talk, you're making an electronic leap of faith with the hope that your intention will be understood. Unfortunately, that original intention may be misinterpreted and mutated into a very different beast. There's a reason why the most important questions — like "Will you marry me?" — are spoken, not tweeted or emailed. Because when you *mean* it, you *say* it and if at all possible you say it face to face.

The Impact of "Live" Communication

If your message is important, pick up the phone. If you have to deliver bad news, make an appointment. If you really care about the person you're communicating with, look them in the eye. Leave email to online receipts, airline check-in procedures, and confirming your attendance to the Straight Talk party.

Remember, *texting is not talking* and *email is not dialogue.* It's essential to business and just as critical in your personal relationships. People want to spend time with people they understand and like, not those whose electronic messages come across like spam.

If you say something in person and your listener doesn't agree, you see it on their faces or feel the vibrations of non-verbal warning bells. When you resort to all things email, that visibility is lost. It may take a not-so-small meltdown or disaster before you see that your burst of acronyms and poorly constructed sentences has created an avalanche that's heading right back in your direction. With some practice and a heightened sense of awareness, you'll learn to better read the reaction of your audience.

People in the highest positions of authority achieve more without tweeting, emailing, texting, or blogging for a very simple reason: *They're less interested in sounding smart and more committed to making their expectations clear.* They seldom rely on an email substitute, but communicate directly, personally, and often one to one. They may use email or blogs to *reinforce* messages, but always as a supplement — it's never a replacement for Straight Talk. The more important the message and the more senior your role, the more critical it becomes to be understood. And most of today's communication "conveniences" are loaded with risks for confusion. Grandma, the Master of Smart Talk, was seldom misunderstood, and she's never touched a keyboard.

Let's not forget, more than 70% of communication is non-verbal. Meaning isn't just in what we say or write. The tone and rhythm of our communication, our expressions, and our gestures are the forgotten elements that make our messages truly meaningful and memorable. Non-verbal communication creates feelings, connections, and lasting impressions. This is essential when we're delivering information that is critical or necessary.

Email presents fertile ground for Smart Talk Traps and other communication gaffes. I strongly recommend *The Dirty Dozen Rules of Email Etiquette,* by the straight-talking Tim Sanders, if you use email as your primary communication. His research will save you an endless amount of time, productivity, and drama at work, at home, and among acquaintances. (www.timsanders.com).

If You Can't Say It, Write It

If you *must* send a message, consider actually writing a letter. For starters, your message is more likely to be received with positive emotion and prioritized near the top of the to-do pile. A handwritten note has become the exception and not the rule, and as we know, nothing stands out like a positive exception. If you want to be just like everybody else, text it. But if you want to be *remembered,* reach for a pen.

How to Apply Straight Talk Principle #2:
Be Obvious and Keep It Simple

This Straight Talk Principle is about being *clear, specific,* and *uncomplicated.*

- Starting today, whenever you communicate, make sure your listeners understand your intentions and the outcomes you're seeking. If you're not sure, ask them.

- Get to the point quickly. Brevity is best.

- Communicate in person. If you can't, use the same keep-it-simple techniques in electronic messages but by all means do use complete sentences!

- Use email, text, and tweets only as a rein-forcement — never as a substitute for direct contact with your intended audience.

"Simplicity is the ultimate sophistication."

Leonardo da Vinci

What the Research Reveals

The *Washington Post* reported the results of a 2011 study at New York University and the University of Basel in Switzerland on one of the dangers of overusing business jargon — that using jargon may make the speaker look like a liar. The study showed that, when you want to seem believable and trustworthy, concrete language is the way to go. People were asked to rate the truthfulness of two sentences that meant the same thing but were worded differently. In the majority of cases, responders said the sentences with the simplest language were true. The researchers determined several reasons why *easy* equals *believable:*

- Our minds process concrete statements more quickly, and we automatically associate *quick and easy* with *true*.

- We can create mental pictures of concrete statements more easily. When something is easier to picture, it's easier to recall, so it seems more true.

- When something is more easily pictured, it seems more plausible, so it's more readily believed. (Hence the value of reinforcement through images, including cartoons.)

If you want people to believe you, the study's authors suggest, stick to simple language that's easy to visualize — concrete verbs like "write" or "walk" are always better than ambiguous ones like "benefit" and "improve."

CHAPTER  3

My Way is Not the Only Way

"Respect a man, and he will do all the more."

John Wooden

FRANK SINATRA was an artist of epic scale and I'm a big fan of his crooning style. *My Way* is a classic, and many have fallen for the allure of declaring that "you did it your way." However, the Chairman of the Board, as he was often referred to, was hardly a productivity or relationship specialist. I'm here to remind you that "my way" is not the *only* way.

The great little parable below is the perfect introduction to the third Smart Talk Trap. It's been cited in serious books and also emerges regularly, with new flavors, on the Internet.

> A large U.S. battleship was communicating with their Canadian allies off the coast of Newfoundland. The Canadians told the U.S. vessel to divert its course by 15 degrees to the south to avoid a collision. The captain of the U.S. ship curtly responded, "Recommend *you* divert *your* course 15 degrees north."

> The Canadians quickly replied that it was absolutely necessary that the U.S. ship shift 15 degrees south. This second request was apparently too much for the feisty American captain, who barked back, "This is the captain of a U.S. Navy battleship, the largest in the Atlantic fleet! We are accompanied by three destroyers, three cruisers, and numerous support vessels. I demand that *you* change *your* course 15 degrees north, or you'll force me to take measures to ensure the safety of this fleet!"

> After a short silence, the Canadians simply responded, "Your call, sir. We're sitting in a lighthouse."

Sow Smart, Reap Smart

It takes no superior intellect or extensive experience in living to understand and believe that what goes around comes around. Call it karma. Fate. Destiny. But for some reason, we continue to struggle with the irrefutable law that we must offer sincere respect in order to get genuine respect in return. Respect is the alchemy behind the Straight Talk Principle we'll now explore.

Despite countless lessons throughout history, as a species, we simply haven't absorbed the message, "What we sow, we shall reap." There are no exceptions — we attract what we cultivate and project; we ultimately get what we've earned.

A Straight *Jerk* is not a Straight *Talker*

Now, be careful — if you don't do this right, you can actually practice Straight Talk without achieving any of its benefits. Read on!

I once worked with a CEO who was a brilliant engineer, a charismatic speaker, and a successful entrepreneur. Anyone who met him could see that he was a Straight Talker. By simply cutting to the point and keeping his intentions and directions clear, he could rouse audiences and inspire his staff to increase their productivity.

But even as he was well on his way to greater success, he couldn't shake this particular Smart Talk Trap — that *his* way was not just the *best* way, but the *only* way. While he said what he meant and never waxed philosophical, he was a pro at blind arrogance. He operated as a tyrant most of the time. He could have used his natural talents and abilities to encourage greater achievement in others, create natural loyalty and commitment to a mission, and develop the very people who could make him more successful. But instead, he chose to climb atop his self-inflated ego and condescendingly issue commands. Granted, they were *clear* commands, but they failed to include the *respect* that was badly needed. His house of cards was starting to sway.

> This CEO could have used his abilities to develop his staff. But he chose to climb atop his self-inflated ego and condescendingly issue commands.

After a short run of success, his professional and personal achievements crashed and burned. What goes around *did* come back around. If you find yourself valuing your time above that of the people who work for you, brace yourself for a dramatic reduction in

> If you value your time above the time of those who work for you, brace yourself for a reduction in engagement and loyalty...and a hard landing.

engagement and loyalty. Leaders at home, at s̷
the office, or in government who operate as if they ai̷
above the law because "they know better" and "they
are right" will always fail. It may take months, years
or even decades, but you will fall and it will be a hard
landing. Blind arrogance always turns on its host. It's
just a matter of time.

Straight Talk Principle #3

The third Straight Talk Principle is *Be Open-Minded
and Respectful.* Straight Talk is never rude, arrogant,
or personal. It's also non-emotional.

We've all dealt with someone who just has to
"have it their way." Even if "their way" is adequate
most of the time, is it truly the *only* way or the *best*
way? With 94 good years under her belt, Grandma
Adeline has earned the right to demand things "her
way," and she certainly has her preferences and routine. But I've lost count of the times when this wise
sage said, "I learned something new today." Grass
doesn't grow on a busy street, so keep yourself busy
by learning something new.

We live in a world that can connect ideas and
thoughts in seconds with a simple Google search. More
than ever before, we should embrace the options at
our disposal to cultivate new ideas and new connections. As arrogant as "my way or the highway" was

in the past, it's implication is even more dangerous today. It's a statement of ignorance.

Don't be confused by short-term success that's won by arrogance, bullying, or detraction. There are many ways to craft a short-term run, but only the businesses, relationships, and innovations that are built on credible foundations will survive. In business, the math has to work in order to survive. In science, the formulas must be understood and applied. The only way to produce lasting results and success is to be sure that conversations are genuinely kind and without ill intention. Benjamin Disraeli, a former British Prime Minister was practicing Straight Talk when he said, "It is always easier to be critical than to be correct." Grandma would often quip: "I'm not saying anything if I don't have something nice to say." Fairness and a touch of humility in our treatment of others is the basis for creating lasting success, productivity, and harmony.

> The only way to produce lasting results and success is to be sure that conversations are genuinely kind and without ill intention.

The concept of being open-minded, respectful, and non-emotional in dealing with others is universally necessary to all roles and in all cultures. Grandma Adeline repeated two scenarios that we will face in our lives and she stressed that how we handle these scenarios will produce dramatically different results.

+ When you have an opportunity to praise someone, it may be acceptable to do it in a public way.
+ When you have a need to criticize or coach, do it in private. Doing otherwise, intentionally or through neglect, violates this Straight Talk Principle. It creates an emotional and often negative and defensive communication environment. And such an environment is never productive to achieving personal or group goals.

How to Apply Straight Talk Principle #3: Be Open-Minded and Respectful

This Straight Talk Principle reminds us to *respect others and remain open-minded.*

- Today, don't allow an unkind, malicious, or negative comment to be said without objecting, respectfully of course.

- Act respectful to others and notice what happens around you. If you view people with respect, you may see a change in those you're speaking *to* as well as those you're speaking *about.* Max Planck, Nobel Prize recipient, pointed the way when he encouraged, "When we change the way we look at something, the thing we look upon will change." Our approach and disposition to a subject actually influences the possible outcomes.

- When you feel the urge to respond emotionally, think first, then phrase your comment in a clear, open-minded way.

> "Always be kind, for everyone is fighting a hard battle."
>
> *Plato*

What the Research Reveals

In 2011, the Rotterdam School of Management studied the area of "respectful leadership." After polling employees, researchers determined several behaviors that determined "respectful leadership."

Some behaviors were easily predictable, such as "Recognizes my work" and "Treats me in a fair manner." But others were more connected to the language a person uses. They included:

- Expresses criticism in an objective and constructive way.

- Shows a genuine interest in my opinions and assessments.

- Provides information that is relevant to me.

- Interacts in an open and honest way.

They also determined that receiving respectful treatment from a superior makes people feel very group-oriented. This encourages people to spread their own respectfulness not just to those who gave them respect, but to their entire group or team.

In their recommendations to leaders, researchers questioned the notion that if leaders treat employees with too much respect, their effectiveness is weakened.

This study showed that when leaders respect others, it's much easier for people to identify with and follow them.

The researchers noted that conversation is a powerful means of showing respect: "If I want to talk to you, it's because I believe you have something valuable to say."

The group concluded that respectful leadership can make an organization a great place to work, and that a happy, stable workforce contributes to reduced costs and improved performance.

Reported by Niels van Quaquebeke, business professor at Erasmus University.

Erica Pinsky works with organizations to build respectful and inclusive workplace cultures that attract and retain quality employees. She has studied the field of respect for decades, and her research shows that employees who feel disrespected spend up to <u>50% of their work time dealing with the effects of that disrespect</u>, which means a serious productivity problem for any business. She has found that most people don't do anything to stop the disrespect, as they "hate confrontation." Pinsky says this means that confrontation avoidance, not conversation, can become the norm in those workplaces. As a result, "Issues that are interfering with an individual's ability to do their job well, to achieve their full potential and contribute to the success of the business are not being dealt with, and that silence is slowly killing any chance for top-employer status" — not to mention pursuit of improving employee engagement and organizational productivity.

Erica Pinsky is the author of *Road to Respect, Path to Profit.* See www.ericajpinskyinc.com.ca.

CHAPTER  4

Beware the Empty Suit

"Just be what you are and speak from your guts and heart — it's all you have."

Hubert Humphrey

I HAVE VIVID MEMORIES of Grandma Adeline walking here, there, and everywhere to lend a helpful hand to her family and friends. She was always on the move and always driven by a sense of accountability to help those around her. I'd often ask, "Who are you off to help today, Grandma?" She'd respond, "Who? I ain't no owl! It doesn't matter who. What matters is that we get up in the morning and do something useful!"

Grandma always encouraged us never to ask *who will help us* but rather to ask *who we intend to help* with our gifts and talents. She has always demonstrated this accountability, with the right attitude and the right actions.

Alan Greenspan, retired chairman of the Federal Reserve Bank, agrees with her perspective. He once said, "I have found no greater satisfaction than achieving success through honest dealing and strict adherence to the view that, for you to gain, those you deal with should gain as well."

Is Your Suit Empty?

This disposition for serving isn't just a powerful guidepost. It also creates a distinction between holding ourselves truly *accountable* for a conversation or cause and simply *participating* in it. This is a deeply important distinction, and we need to understand it regardless of our calling, career, or state in life.

> Talking about something, someone, or some issue without being clear on your position is a Smart Talk Trap.

In the corporate world, we separate the "empty suits" from the "real deals" based on the measurement of self-accountability. If you're sitting on the sidelines offering a whole lot of Smart Talk but taking no measurable accountability for the outcomes of the discussion, you're an empty suit. "Talking about" something, someone, or some issue without being clear on your position, your commitment, or your own accountability is one of the most widespread Smart Talk Traps I've witnessed. Sadly, we can find this behavior practised in any area of life, from those who provide service in a retail shop to those who sell bonds on the trading floor. Frankly, an "empty suit" is much too polite a label — because if you're operating like an empty suit, you're nothing more than a *fraud*.

Pointless Chatter

When we perpetually sit on the sidelines — at the dinner table or in the boardroom — critiquing, criticizing, or complaining without taking ownership for an outcome, we're contributing to the Smart Talk epidemic. Every discussion doesn't have to end in a balanced scorecard or a report, but if you find yourself participating in conversations that never lead to outcomes, save yourself the time and energy and call a time out! You're on a dead-end road to achieving nothing.

One of the most frequent opening lines that Smart Talkers use is, "Let me play devil's advocate with you…" When you hear this, listen very carefully for the words that follow. See if you can figure out what the speaker is personally committed to and how much he's truly willing to support an idea, project, or initiative that originated with someone else. We have the right to ask for clarity. We have the right and *obligation* to disagree if we oppose an idea. But we shouldn't waste time masking a lack of agreement or a lack of alignment with mundane expressions of support and feigned interest. When you do this, yes, you know the answer. You're a fraud.

Take Your Part in the Cast

This leads us from accountability to *authenticity*. Life is too short and work is generally challenging enough, so dealing with people who refuse to authentically play their part is a real chore. Each day, we're in a play called "Life" for which there are no rehearsals, and it's a pain to drag along detached cast members. We need to commit to playing our part authentically rather than just showing up for a role. No one appreciates a lackluster performance whether it's on stage, on a playing field, in a sales meeting, or in a classroom.

> If we are unwilling to ask, "What can I do?" we are worse than a detached cast member. We are an empty suit.

In any situation, if we are unwilling to ask, "What can I do? What is the accountability of my role?" we are worse than a detached cast member. We are an empty suit. Determining the distinction between a real, accountable participant and a living, breathing fraud is essential. Want some examples?

- ✦ The coach who refuses to take accountability for the perverted crimes of his staff is a fraud.
- ✦ The chief executive who launches a new strategy for shareholders, partners, and employees to follow, while planning a personal exit from the business is a fraud.
- ✦ The teacher who abuses power to manipulate students for personal gain is a fraud.
- ✦ Parents who preach the laws of ethical, clean living to their children but violate those same principles personally are frauds.
- ✦ The spiritual leader who quotes from sacred books and inspired Teachers and then condones violence is a fraud.
- ✦ The team captain who blames everyone but himself for losing a game is a fraud.

Curse You, Alex Trebek!

Now, there are times when we don't offer a solution or suggestion because, frankly, we don't know the answer! A big part of being authentic is being honest about *what you don't know.*

However, some remain tempted, even *desperate* to have the answer to everything. Decades of *Jeopardy* and other such game shows may be to blame. Of course, a person has to be smart just to get on the show, but despite everything socked away in the brain of Joe Contestant, his re-occurring nightmare is pressing the buzzer and blurting out a wrong answer on prime time TV. If Joe goes home a loser, he'll wear the badge of "Village Idiot" for the rest of his life, right? Maybe not.

> A big part of being authentic is being honest about *what you don't know.*

Life can be a bit like the game show world. We have placed the highest premium on having the right answer *now* (even in the form of a question). But we all know that at times we *don't* have the best answer in the moment. How can it be that thousands of *Jeopardy losers* have gone on to live productive lives? In fact, they may actually be the "winners" because they've learned the value and power of saying, "I don't know." They know that the real "idiot" is the person who persists in *pretending* they are right.

The Power of "I Don't Know"
You will find great power in those three words. Imagine a world where people didn't feel pressured to have the right answer all the time — or the one prescribed by some expert. Surely there are instances where more

than one answer is right. What if there was a game show where the answers were possibilities?

The promotion of possibilities is a powerful distinction for Straight Talkers because it invites people to generate new ideas, seek opinions, respect the input of others and, in general, reach for something bigger and better than today's sanitized answers.

So what's holding us back from the simple statement, "I don't know"? If you're committed to being authentic, these words need to be a big part of your vocabulary. Not only do they represent honest Straight Talk, but they also have a special power to create value. They have power because they clear away illusions for you and for your audience, and they also empower others to offer their own versions of what is possible. They have value because they eliminate wasted time and effort trying to prove that your answer is the only "right answer."

> The words "I don't know" are honest and authentic. They empower others to offer their own versions of what is possible.

The next time you don't know, just say it. Watch for the reaction. If you're a well-known "black belt" Smart Talker, be prepared for people to fall out of their chairs or stammer to fill the silence. They've probably been conditioned to expect an earful from you to every question raised. Your empty suit will be on its way to the cleaners, permanently.

Now, if "I don't knows" start stacking up for you, it's clearly time to evaluate whether you're in the right role, if you require some skills development or frankly to check if you're paying attention. You can't "I don't know" yourself to the top of your profession if you truly lack knowledge or experience. Your commitment to being authentic, first and foremost with yourself, will help you make the distinction between, "I need to be clear — I don't have the answer," and "It is clear that I have too few answers, so I might be in the wrong job or I may be more dependent on the support of others than I care to admit." As with all the Straight Talk Principles, don't fake it and don't abuse it. The principles will increase clarity, productivity, and meaning but only if you're sincere in their use.

Straight Talk Principle #4

The fourth Straight Talk Principle is *Be Accountable and be Authentic.*

Have you caught yourself in the "empty suit" Smart Talk Trap? If so, commit to demonstrating your personal accountability and authenticity at the earliest opportunity! It really does get easier with practice.

Even Grandma is unafraid to admit, "I'm not sure, Danny." So authentic is her communication and intent that, over the years, I've learned the telltale signs that this answer is coming because Grandma shakes her head and rubs her hands simultaneously. It's the body language that precedes the honesty that I've come to rely on and that I seek to emulate.

On many occasions, I've had the opportunity when working with someone as their "coach" to practice this principle by acknowledging, "I don't really know." I'll never forget the first time I exercised this principle in a coaching session. Consider the relationship expectations between a coach and player, a parent and a child, or a mentor and a fellow colleague. It would be easy to assume that the coach or mentor must *always* have the answer to the problem or topic. But that would be pure ego talking.

> It would be easy to assume that the coach or mentor must *always* have the answer. But that would be pure ego talking.

The first time I practiced this principle professionally, I shared openly that I had neither personal experience nor a very good answer for how to deal with a particular personal tragedy. The reaction I received spoke volumes! At first, I saw a look of surprise because the assumption may have been, "As my coach, you *must* have all the answers." But when I followed up with, "I have a friend who went through a similar (life) crisis, and he may be willing to talk with you about how he dealt with similar feelings and questions," the temporary surprise led to a relaxed and more engaging discussion. It was as if we had granted each other permission to talk without boundaries, to brainstorm without a conclusion, and at the end of the day what this person really needed from me was a willingness to listen and empathize.

My openness reinforced that we had a *relationship of equals*, regardless of who was coaching. Our collaboration strengthened and my colleague thanked me then and afterward for acknowledging that I didn't always have the answers. She said that she wasn't expecting me to have shared a similar experience but she asked me the question because I was a good listener and I demonstrated I cared about her as a person.

As Lao Tzu coached, "True nobility is not about being better than others. It is about being better than you used to be." We can practice being better than we used to be by applying the fourth Straight Talk Principle consistently.

How to Apply Straight Talk Principle #4:
Be Accountable and Be Authentic

This Straight Talk Principle reminds us to be authentic and to bear our share of responsibility in every role we take on.

- Determine what you really believe, and don't be afraid to stand up for it in a respectful manner.
- Be responsible for your own actions, whether you're acting alone or as part of a "cast."
- Start saying, "I don't know" when it's the truth.
- Realize that you don't have to have all the answers yourself. It's a great relief and it opens the door to new possibilities.

"If you cannot find the truth right where you are, where else do you expect to find it?"

Ralph Waldo Emerson

What the Research Reveals

Bill George, Harvard Business School professor and former CEO of MedTronic, is a recognized authority on authenticity in business leadership. A few years ago, he teamed with researchers Peter Sims, Andrew N. McLean, and Diana Mayer to conduct a study of 125 leaders to answer the question, "How can people become and remain authentic leaders?" They interviewed a wide range of people from a variety of backgrounds. Half were CEOs and the other half were in various stages of career leadership.

In a nutshell, the findings showed that these people had no universal characteristics. Their leadership styles resulted from their individual life stories. They had made a practice of self-testing through daily challenges and constant consideration of who they truly were. As they did so, they defined their own leadership and saw how being real made them more effective.

The research team found these results "extremely encouraging," as they reinforced that a person need not be a "born leader." They concluded that self-knowledge is a natural path to understanding how to lead: "You can learn from others' experiences, but there is no way you can be successful when you are trying to be like them. People trust you when you are genuine and authentic, not a replica of someone else...You need to be who you are, not try to emulate somebody else."

In *Authentic Leadership: Rediscovering the Secrets to Creating Lasting Value* (Jossey-Bass), George writes, "Authentic leaders demonstrate a passion for their purpose, practice their values consistently, and lead with their hearts as well as their heads. They establish long-term, meaningful relationships and have the self-discipline to get results. They know who they are."

For further reading: *True North: Discover Your Authentic Leadership* by Bill George with Peter Sims (Jossey-Bass).

CHAPTER  5

Pride Goeth Before Each Fall

"Conceit is the quicksand of success."

Arnold Glasow

ONE OF THE GREATEST military failures in modern history came at the direction of U.S. President John F. Kennedy. At the time, Kennedy enjoyed the highest approval ratings and popularity of any modern head of state, with a personality and appeal that extended well beyond the borders of his country. He was truly the fair-haired leader with the golden touch and almost universal appeal.

However, in 1961, Kennedy ordered an invasion of Cuba that historians still consider a colossal disaster.

But in the wake of this failing as commander-in-chief, Kennedy did something profound — something that actually *drove up* his appeal rating with American citizens. To the amazement of pollsters, Kennedy took swift and complete accountability for the failure. He didn't blame any other person on his staff or any other government department. He didn't get philosophical about his intentions or blame the "best-laid plans" theory. He deliberately and quickly took responsibility for the decisions, the failed outcome, and the resulting side effects. Although Kennedy was not the first globally recognized leader to reach a pre-crisis zenith of popularity, his willingness to demonstrate that he was vulnerable and accountable reinforced his popularity and his credibility in a way that was not anticipated.

> In the wake of this failing, Kennedy did something that actually *drove up* his appeal rating with Americans.

This brave action is a clear guidepost for a leader of any kind. When we take full and unfiltered responsibility for our actions — especially our mistakes and miscues — we demonstrate a level of vulnerability and humility that actually generates *more* support and *more* credibility from those around us. Equally important, this lesson applies even to those not in a position of leadership. We all have opportunities to direct a project, lead a conversation, initiate some action, or actively participate on a team. All roles, personal and professional, can benefit from a dose of genuine humility.

A Lack of Vulnerability Can Be Dangerous!

Humility is a virtue that can be applied to improve productivity and understanding and it may actually be essential to your health! A Gallup study of 3,000 workers in Sweden found that those who considered their manager "very incompetent" had a 24% higher risk of serious heart problems. Shockingly, after four years under the same conditions, the risk of serious heart issues jumped to 39%! If we don't ask for help, we not only hurt ourselves, we become a negative influence on the well-being of those who work for us.

Incompetence is as dangerous as poor diet or genetic defects. If we are lacking in skills or knowledge, we must ask for help and develop the competencies required, regardless of our role or title. Leaders are not above the rule to demonstrate some vulnerability. Ask for help, feedback, or opinions — especially if you're traveling in uncharted waters or if the outcome of your decisions will affect the long-term good of your constituents. Your pride may not only

> Leaders are not above the rule. Ask for feedback, especially if you're traveling in uncharted waters.

bring about your decline (and it surely will) but it may also inflict health risks on others. So if you find yourself working with or for gross incompetence, beware. If the incompetent leader is blind to their shortcomings and deaf to your offers to assist, follow the advice of Gandalf to Frodo and his companions: "Fly, you fools!", and get out of harm's way. Your very health and well-being are at stake, not to mention the credibility and effectiveness of the organization that keeps incompetent clowns as ringleaders. Commit to help someone down the path of development or toward improvement or get off the boat they're steering. Their incompetence will surely find the rocky coast or the iceberg to the detriment of all. If you find yourself clowning about, acknowledge your blind spots or shortcoming and seek the help and support you need to deliver the value expected of you in your role.

It does take Courage

Vulnerability and leadership are seldom linked in most business environments, and there are many countries and cultures where this concept is still challenged. I've been traveling the world for 20 years and, without question, there are cultures where the mere thought of expressing vulnerability is anathema, especially

> Leaders can learn from their peers about the power of engaging people at a deeper level through healthy transparency.

for those in positions of authority. But I've also seen some traditional cultures and norms starting to change and a certain degree of transparency is being introduced. Why? Because even the most rigid traditions must adapt and evolve to survive. With the advent of instantaneous communication and access to information, leaders can learn from their peers about the power of engaging constituents, employees, family, or friends at a deeper level through healthy transparency.

A "Good Pain"

However, with vulnerability comes some pain. I've found that the strongest resistance to this healthy pain comes from those who care most about their titles and positions, and less for their constituents or commitments they've made. I wish I had a camera every time I've introduced this principle of vulnerability, especially to people in a clear position of leadership. The facial reactions are priceless! Imagine a child biting into a lemon for the first time or dipping a pickle into a glass of milk. Their expressions range from utter surprise to a comical grimace.

Most people — but in particular, leaders — find this principle not only surprising but painful! This is because they mistakenly connect "vulnerable" with "weak." They are certain that they haven't worked this hard, caffeinated their way through the best schools, and endured years of climbing the corporate ladder only to reveal the soft side of their impenetrable armor! They've convinced themselves of their own omnipotence, and they're not about to let down their guard. But the so-called pain that comes from allowing ourselves to be vulnerable is the kind that comes naturally when we grow and develop new muscle strength and stretch for something better.

Rule Number Six

The brilliant Ben Zander, orchestra conductor and celebrated public speaker, often tells a story that cuts to the heart of this Straight Talk Principle.

Two prime ministers planned to meet at the embassy for lunch. Just as they began their discussion, a staff member of the host burst into the room, agitated about an unexpected scheduling conflict. The prime minister said gently, "Peter, please remember Rule Number Six." Just as suddenly as he had arrived, Peter composed himself, apologized to the prime minister and his visitor, and left the room.

Not long afterward, there was a knock at the door, followed by another interruption. A different staffer launched into a frustrated outburst about a problem with a co-worker. Once, again, the hosting prime minister simply said, "Maria, please remember

Rule Number Six." Maria also quickly apologized and excused herself.

Although the visiting prime minister had witnessed the first interruption without comment, he could no longer contain his curiosity. He said, "Pray tell — what is Rule Number Six?" The host replied, "It really is quite simple. 'Don't take yourself so darned seriously.'" The visitor laughed and was suitably impressed, clearly intent on introducing the rule to his own staff.

When the lunch meeting concluded, he asked his host, "If you don't mind sharing your secrets, what are the other rules?" With a smile, the gracious host responded, "There are no other rules!"

Humility vs. Pride

I have found Rule Number Six to be universally applicable, starting with me, myself, I and extending to the countless people I've met, especially those I've had the privilege of coaching. If we would just step down from our pedestals of self importance and acknowledge that *our* point of view, *our* convictions, and *our* priorities are not the center of the universe, we can gain a much-needed perspective on our thoughts and actions.

We can identify those who resist vulnerability at all costs as egomaniacs or simply unreasonably stubborn. If this might be you, try to discard your ego and pride and you'll be rewarded with the ability to move on from failure more quickly and return your focus to productive behavior and activity. Smart Talkers consistently fail to do this. Instead, they double up on their Smart Talk in a fierce attempt to cover up the obvious, often reaching a state of denial that keeps them from realizing what everyone else already knows: *You goofed! You missed the mark. You made a mistake.* What a surprise. You're human! Cut the Smart Talk and save yourself some energy and self-respect.

> Smart Talkers double up on Smart Talk to cover up what everyone else already knows: *You goofed!*

The opposite of humility is, of course, pride. Now, we've all been warned that "Pride goeth before a fall" but have we really made note of the consequences? Grandma has her own take on this. She calls it "SPS." I heard this acronym for the first time decades ago after we'd stopped to talk with one of her "lady friends" at the post office. After five minutes of listening to this woman boast about her recent triumphs, Grandma pulled me close enough to hear her whisper, "SPS." When we moved on, I asked her what she meant. "Self-Praise Stinks," she said with a laugh. Her message is timeless and serves to remind us that pride is not only a trap but a relative of arrogance — which you'll find has no friends.

I often think about the examples Grandma shared with me through the very way she lives her life. Her willingness to be open still draws people from near and far to consult with her — family and friends, and even former employers and their children! All find inspiration and good counsel at Grandma's kitchen table.

And yet, one of the most remarkable facts about her life is how she demonstrates her own vulnerability. She's an open book about the things that keep her up at night: fear of the dark, fear of losing her eyesight, fear of being left alone, fear of ending up in a retirement home. The very fact that she chooses to reveal her own Achilles' heel helps others to share their fears and concerns without hesitation. Her wisdom and determination, paired with her tirelessness in connecting deeply with others, makes everyone feel that she's *their* grandmother too. They not only respect her, but they *know* her. Whether the beneficiary of Grandma's pearls of wisdom is 5 years old or 75 years young, they know the fears that she personally stares down. They witness the right dosage of vulnerability that creates comfort and reassurance. Grandma has always been quick to say, "I ain't no saint." This is her simple yet effective way to discard any pride that may be surfacing or distracting her from the opportunity to serve others without judgement.

🗨 **Straight Talk Principle #5**

The fifth Straight Talk Principle is *Be Vulnerable and Pocket Your Pride.* Vulnerability has two requirements: It must be *"context-aware"* and it must be *sincere.*

Context — the place, time, and audience — is an important consideration because there are times when people are genuinely looking for you to take a stand, lead from the front, or declare the "next steps." All of these can be accomplished without sacrificing this principle, but vulnerability can't be an excuse to avoid action.

Vulnerability must also be sincere. We should show a willingness to learn from and acknowledge our errors and deficits without divesting our responsibility. And we need to do this in a way that makes sense to our audience, whether that's an individual or a roomful of eager followers.

> The moment vulnerability is overused or fabricated, it will become the nail in your credibility coffin.

The moment vulnerability is overused or fabricated, it not only loses its sincerity and effect, but it will become the nail in your credibility coffin. Let's face it — no one is interested in following people who constantly dwell on their own blind spots and shortcomings! And few people can make any progress on their pursuits if they perpetually flog themselves over areas to improve.

The important distinction is to take *clear ownership* for major missteps, judgment errors, or lack of knowledge or experience we may be wrestling with. This allows us to quickly turn attention and energy toward finding a solution instead of wasting time (and your credibility) avoiding accountability or searching for a scapegoat.

You Can't Fake It

It's useless and counterproductive to fake vulnerability or accountability. People can spot a counterfeit a mile away! I can't say this strongly enough: *Be sure you are really ready to be transparent, clear, and non-emotional about what you say.* Get a coach, or ask a friend to be a sounding board so you can practice, if necessary. But *do not, under any circumstances, pretend to act accountable* because you think this will solve all your problems. You must be committed to pocketing your pride with sincerity so you can experience the true release of discarding Smart Talk overhead and appreciate the support that will follow when you demonstrate sincere vulnerability.

Whether you're leading a congregation, a classroom of teenagers, a boardroom, or a ball club, a touch of authentic transparency can make the difference between simple engagement and determined loyalty, between involvement and unquestionable commitment. We can take a lesson from former U.S. President, Ronald Reagan, who said, "Anything is possible when you have no care for who gets the credit."

A Tip for the Wary

If you're long on self-confidence but have trouble digesting the idea of expressing vulnerability, here's a recommendation free of charge. Take a step toward recovery and boost your real self-worth by sharing your knowledge, experience, and a taste of your confidence by coaching someone. When you turn your attention outward to help and develop others, you're *required* to demonstrate a level of emotional intelligence that allows you to put someone else or the greater good ahead of your own ego.

You will also inevitably learn some things about yourself and spot your own areas for improvement as you transfer the skills, knowledge, or experience that "make you great" to someone else. There is no better antidote for pride than the patience required to step back from our own pursuits long enough to help someone else advance their ideas and their development.

Herve Wiener offers a thought that helps us remember to pocket our pride: "When the peacock struts his stuff, he shows his backside to half the world." Enough said?

**How to Apply Straight Talk Principle #5:
Be Vulnerable and Pocket Your Pride**

This Straight Talk Principle prescribes *vulnerability* and *humility*.

- Remember SPS — "Self-Praise Stinks."
- Take responsibility for all your actions, and you'll get more support and earn credibility.
- Live with Rule Number Six by your side. Don't take yourself so seriously!
- When you dump your ego and pride, you can get back to productive behavior far more quickly.

"In the beginning, people think vulnerability will make you weak, but it does the opposite. It shows you're strong enough to care."

Victoria Pratt

What the Research Reveals

Brené Brown, a research professor at the University of Houston, studies vulnerability, courage, worthiness, and shame. Brown was interviewed by *Fast Company* in 2012 on "Why Doing Awesome Work Means Making Yourself Vulnerable." The result of her research in this area has produced some marvelous revelations about the role of vulnerability in producing great leaders and great results. This is what she concluded:

- Vulnerability means uncertainty, risk, and emotional exposure.

- Vulnerability is the glue that binds relationships together. <u>Leaders are called upon to model the vulnerability they want to see in their people</u>. This means we have to model taking risks and failing.

- Vulnerability is also the birthplace of innovation and creativity. I challenge anyone to point to any act of innovation that was not born of vulnerability — putting an idea on a table that half the people in the room thought was stupid. If the idea makes sense to everyone right away, there's nothing innovative about it!

- Vulnerability is showing up and being seen. I can't think of a single leader who doesn't want that from their people. Just showing up requires a lot of courage.

For further reading: *Daring Greatly: How the Courage to Be Vulnerable Transforms the Way We Live, Love, Parent, and Lead* by Brené Brown (2012).

CHAPTER 6

Calumny Is for Cowards and Detraction Is for Deadbeats

"There is no readier way for a man to bring his own worth into question than by endeavoring to detract from the worth of other men."

John Tillotson

Smart Talking isn't only about words that are meaningless, conversations without accountability, or tirades in the boardroom. The Smart Talking epidemic is fueled by cowards — yes, *cowards* — who spend their time talking behind people's backs. One of the most cancerous Smart Talk Traps is detraction — speaking ill about others without content or context but solely with the intent to damage another's reputation. A detractor is a Smart Talker at the top of the offender's list.

Sadly, this Smart Talk Trap is learned and practiced in school cafeterias, at family dinner tables, and at neighborhood barbeques. And of course, it's a staple in many corporations. How many times have you been party to these kinds of conversations? Does this happen frequently? Daily? More often than that? If you're unwilling to share constructive feedback directly with an individual, hit the pause button on your vocal cords and refrain!

When someone attempts to lure Grandma into a gossip session, her pet phrase is, "I ain't saying nothing." Mind you, this doesn't mean for one second that she has no opinion (and often a strong and reasoned one), but she taught us never to confuse *the right to an opinion* with the *good sense to keep it to ourselves*. She taught us that there's a time and a place to step up to the microphone, but to do it carelessly is to create havoc. Sadly, most of us can recall countless examples when personal and organizational reputations were not only tarnished but materially damaged in the media without

> Never confuse the right to an opinion with the good sense to keep it to yourself.

due process. It's a sad commentary that so many of us are willing to slander our neighbors, run a colleague's reputation into the ground, or disparage someone just because we don't share the same opinions.

Detraction Has Deep Roots

Why do we do this? Well, after learning from Grandma and watching this "detraction disaster" unfold all over the world, I believe I've found the answer: *The fundamental inclination to detract begins with personal insecurity.* Ultimately, it reveals a very shallow character. And the deeper the insecurity, the more rampant and vicious the detraction and calumny.

There's a wonderful fable that illustrates how detraction can be more dangerous than a direct assault.

> A young man once asked his teacher, "Is it worse to strike your fellow man or to say something bad about him behind his back?" In reply, the teacher asked the young man to take two feather pillows to the balcony of his home and wait. He was to drop one pillow onto the first dog that passed by. Then, he was to cut open the second pillow and dump the feathers onto the second dog that passed by. Confused but obedient, the boy went home to follow these directions.

Soon (as there were many dogs in his village) the boy returned. The teacher told him to retrieve the first pillow and find the dog. While the pillow could not harm the dog, the boy was to make amends by offering the dog a treat. After that, the boy was to collect the feathers he had dropped onto the second dog and bring them back in the original pillowcase.

Several hours passed before the student returned, tired and agitated. He collapsed in front of his teacher, and said he had been unable to complete his task. He had found the first dog and made amends. But although he tried very hard, he couldn't retrieve even half the feathers from the second pillow. The breeze had spread them far and wide, and people had crushed them underfoot and kicked them farther afield.

His teacher smiled and said, "There — you have your answer. When we hurt someone directly, we often have an opportunity to make things right if we move quickly and apologize. But when we damage someone's good name, it's like dropping feathers over a balcony. It's impossible to know how quickly

> our words will spread, and equally impossible to retract those negative statements as we can never be sure how far they've traveled. In the end, we can never offer full repair to our fellow man's good name."

Straight Talkers steer clear of these evil twins — detraction and calumny — as they're incompatible with personal integrity. A Straight Talker sees right through lame attempts to cover up the twins by adding a phrase like, "and isn't that a shame." Tacking on, "bless her heart" after tearing down another person's reputation is wasted breath. No one believes these intentions are anything but poison, so we might as well stop faking it. It only exposes the speaker's own insecurity and calls their integrity into question.

Straight Talk Principle #6

The principle that counters this Smart Talk Trap is *Be Courageous and Be Honest.* I've had the pleasure of working with brilliant scientists and engineers, CEOs and entrepreneurs, physicians and teachers. Those who are truly at the top of their profession (and know it) waste no time on detraction. They understand that it serves no purpose. They know that it's not a requirement for their self-confidence, and that it is repulsive to those who practice moral, ethical engagement. William

Arthur Ward expressed what the most successful people practice: "When we seek to discover the best in others, somehow we bring out the best in ourselves."

> Straight Talkers walk away from polluted detraction sessions. They gain no credibility from taking aim at someone's reputation.

If you want to spot a Smart Talker, listen for the person who is quick to jump on the gossip wagon or who loves a good talk behind a neighbor's back. Conversely, Straight Talkers make it clear — verbally and through their choice to walk away from polluted detraction sessions — that they have better things to do and that they gain no credibility from taking aim at someone's reputation.

Many Straight Talkers are guided by a commitment to an ethical code — that to harm another's reputation is morally wrong. Ask any Straight Talker and they'll also confirm their deep belief in the "boomerang" adage, "What goes around comes around." Not only will the boomerang surely return but in the meantime you'll soil your own reputation and risk your own integrity.

Warren Buffet, investment guru and oracle of Omaha, gave his point of view on reputation quite clearly: "If you lose *dollars* for the firm, I will be understanding. If you lose *reputation* for the firm, I will be ruthless." If you speak supportively and refrain

from detraction, you'll preserve your own good reputation and be rewarded with even greater credibility
and success.

If you find yourself falling into the category of
"coward" or "deadbeat," resolve to address this immediately. The habit spreads like
wildfire. People who spread
lies or doubts about others
generally are trying to cover
up their own deep insecurities at any cost — including
the price of someone else's

> The habit can be
> difficult to break and
> may require you to
> address underlying
> insecurities.

reputation. Breaking this habit may require you to
address underlying insecurities, which can take time,
coaching, and encouragement. But let me assure you,
no one wants to waste their time or risk their own
reputation investing in coaching or encouraging a
known detractor. Even those committed to another
person's growth can and often do become targets of
Smart Talk trash.

Habits such as calumny and detraction take time
to develop into a routine. So, too, the counter measure
of Straight Talk Principle #6 will take your focused
attention. But you'll quickly be rewarded with the
gratitude of those around you, who will genuinely place
their trust in you and you'll develop a level of open
communication that was elusive in the past.

Unforgettable People

Those who avoid detraction and practice honest and trustworthy communication are the people we never forget. Several years ago, I worked at a firm that was blessed to have a phenomenal senior recruiting executive on staff. One morning, I arrived at the office to learn that Mike had passed away suddenly overnight, leaving behind a young, beautiful and heart broken family. I remember that day like it was yesterday, as the entire firm numbly made our way through the day. We couldn't fathom closing the gap created by his absence. The pain was more difficult to bear when we thought about Mike's family and that his time with them had been cut so short.

Yet, as we spoke of Mike that day and endless times afterward, one particular virtue emerged that everyone celebrated and, for me, defines a big part of his personal and professional legacy. In all our dealings with Mike, he never uttered a negative comment about another colleague, a candidate, or an associate. He was a true master of Principle #6 and a respected Straight Talker. He understood how to critique a candidate, coach a colleague, and provide constructive feedback to management, but he never crossed the line into detraction or gossip.

The highest form of enlightenment, *to observe without judgment*, was a gift that Mike practiced and shared with all of us. And he left his colleagues and his family with a legacy that included an impeccable reputation as an honest and fair man, and a true role model as colleague, husband, and father.

The practice of this Straight Talk Principle will require conviction and practice, but isn't your own legacy worth the effort?

How to Apply Straight Talk Principle #6: Be Courageous and Be Honest

This Straight Talk Principle is about *speaking to a person instead of about that person,* and about *holding people up instead of talking them down.*

- Starting today, refuse to say anything that detracts from a person's worth, character, or actions.
- Remember the lesson of the feathers — you can never make up for a derogatory remark about someone's character.
- Summon the courage to speak out when you hear unkind words about another person. If you can't, at least walk away from the conversation.

> **"One man cannot hold another man down in the ditch without remaining down in the ditch with him."**
>
> *Booker T. Washington*

What the Research Reveals

In a recent article in *Fast Company,* Mark Goulston, senior vice president of emotional intelligence for Sherwood Partners, said that <u>one of the most important characteristics of effective business leaders is integrity</u>. He recommends never doing anything behind anyone's back, and he added this quote from Mark Twain: "If you tell the truth, you never have to remember anything."

Goulston is the author of *Get Out of Your Own Way: Overcoming Self-Defeating Behavior* (Perigee).

Additionally, Leslie Pratch, president of Pratch & Company in Chicago, wrote a comprehensive study on integrity in business executives. She concluded that showing integrity in business means behaving with a clear set of values that balance self-interest and concern with interest in and concern for others: "Executives who have integrity think about their actions...and how they will affect others. They also think about what they say and how their words will reflect on people's reputations. <u>To be a success in anything you do, develop the competencies and confidence required to stand on your own two feet — not on the reputations of others</u> — to make your sustainable mark."

Leslie Pratch works with companies to assess executives' personality strengths. You can learn more about Leslie and her work at www.pratchco.com

CHAPTER  7

The Essentials: Trust and Consistency

"Trust men and they will be true
to you; trust them greatly, and they
will show themselves great."

Ralph Waldo Emerson

A RECENT STUDY by Mercer Management Consulting revealed that 60% of employees surveyed did not trust that their bosses were communicating with them honestly.

That would confirm that the Smart Talk epidemic is not only rampant, but also ineffective. Who do these Smart Talk clowns think they're fooling? No one! And, of course, this tragedy is not restricted to the corporate world. It's in every walk of life (some more than others) and the outcome will always be the same. Trust — lost. Productivity — lost. Objective of your mission — lost. One of the telltale signs of a Smart Talker is someone who fails the "trust test," and one of the hallmarks of a trustworthy person is consistency. You see, try as they do to keep track of their stories, people who lie are seldom consistent.

> One of the hallmarks of trust is consistency. People who lie are seldom consistent.

You don't have to be a Zen master to practice this Straight Talk Principle, but you do have to develop basic self-discipline so you can sustain harmony in relationships, performance at work, and motivation in the classroom. Straight Talkers are consistent — but you can't be consistent if your life is a rollercoaster of emotions and personality choices.

It Works for the Best

When the most successful people speak about their methods, a common theme is their commitment to consistency. They are not perfect. Some will admit readily to their mistakes and all admit to learning from their mistakes to learn faster and adapt better. The late Steve Jobs offered many personal reflections along these lines. All successful people share a common passion for consistency in fundamental aspects of their life. Whether it's their position on certain issues, their daily routine, or their approach to communication, research, or innovation, they make a habit of practicing *deliberate and consistent approaches*.

The Importance of Discipline

William Arthur Ward accurately stated, "The price of excellence is discipline. The cost of mediocrity is disappointment." Still, many people, especially in Western cultures, bristle at the very mention of self-discipline, as they'd like to believe we've evolved beyond that concept. But they betray themselves and they will find they've jumped on a perilous path. In order to be consistent in speech, planning, and action, we must apply self-discipline.

> "The price of excellence is discipline. The cost of mediocrity is disappointment."
>
> *W. A. Ward*

Grandma would quip, "*Practice* discipline or *be* disciplined," and she grew up in an era where a bit of corporal punishment was encouraged. Teachers may no longer paddle students in many parts of the world, but students' requirement to practice self-discipline will never be out of vogue. Self-discipline creates the strength of character required to be deliberate and consistent in your communications.

 **Straight Talk Principle #7**

This brings us to the seventh Straight Talk Principle: to **Be Deliberate and Consistent.** Why is consistency so important? Because auditors look for it. Shareholders desire it. Athletes practice it. Soup is defined by it! Consistency is an essential part of the formula for sustainable success. Consistency guides businesses when they set policies and guidelines. Consistency allows teachers to manage difficult classrooms fairly and effectively. And the practice of consistent communication creates an environment of trust among friends, family, colleagues, and stakeholders that is essential to realizing peak performance and great results. The most successful parents, athletes, artists, and scientists have learned the secret — that an organized mind, deliberate and consistent, allows them to channel pressure into results. They don't interpret pressure as stress. They use pressure to accelerate innovation and collaboration.

> The most successful people have learned the secret — that an organized mind allows them to channel pressure into results.

The Cost of Inconsistency

The sources of inconsistency — a dangerous Smart Talk Trap — are plentiful. Some are purposeful, some come from neglect, and some are evidence of gross incompetence. This last example is noteworthy. We've all met or worked with people who are simply incompetent in their roles. While these clowns act out a part they clearly can't perform, they wreak havoc on productivity, employee engagement, and customer satisfaction. Incompetence produces volumes of inconsistency, and while all of this is an endless source of lost productivity, the greatest burden is what Stephen M.R. Covey refers to as the "trust tax." *Trust tax is the withdrawal made against your credibility and productivity when you fail to speak, act, and operate truthfully and ethically.* Remember, that which can't be trusted will always smell of Smart Talk. And when trust is broken, the game is over — even if you don't realize it.

> For more on the importance of Trust, including insights into behaviors that develop trust dividends over trust taxes, I highly recommend Stephen M. R. Covey's book, *The Speed of Trust.*

If you find yourself confronted with incompetence, don't neglect your Straight Talk Principles. Your patience may be tested, but your integrity and commitment to Straight Talk will sustain you. And when the clowns move on, your own credibility will still be intact and you'll have a firm foundation necessary to recapture lost productivity.

Consistency Pays Off

Be deliberate and be consistent. When you're *deliberate,* you acknowledge your purpose and intentions openly and without pretense, and you don't apply any sugar-coating. When you're *consistent*, you reinforce "what you see is *really* what you get" and that your "face" reflects your intentions and your commitments.

Need some examples? Birds in flight travel in a consistent formation to dramatically improve their speed and reduce fatigue. The solution for complex equations requires consistent application of formulas. Repeated success on the field of play, in the boardroom, or at home — all rely on consistent execution of the fundamentals. And nowhere is this more important than for those in positions of leadership — parents, pastors, executive chefs, and chief executives.

> Be consistent, and if you adjust your approach based on experience, you remain a Straight Talker.

All great results point to the necessity for deliberate thought and consistent action. This requires self-confidence that is not arrogant, but steady. It doesn't mean you'll never change your mind when new information and feedback is available, and it doesn't mean you're a robot walking through life on one frequency. What it *does* mean is that you adjust your thoughts, approach, and intentions based on experience, input, and learning from past mistakes, and you remain a Straight Talker without pause. You articulate clearly what is important, what has changed, and what is required. You communicate with the same level of consistency and commitment, whether the news is good or bad.

Many of the people I've coached take to this Principle right away because they immediately feel the relief that comes from using a consistent approach to their affairs. They don't have to "fake it" any longer! They don't have to be one way for the boss, one way for their subordinates, and one way for their family! They can soak up the pleasure of being authentically *themselves*.

Don't Abandon Your Principles

This euphoria often carries on unchallenged until we face our first head-on collision with change. When change arrives on the scene, we can find ourselves struggling with how to remain deliberate and consistent, especially when delivering bad news.

This is where the other Straight Talk Principles come home to support Principle #7. These are the times when honest *vulnerability* is tested and, *"I don't know"* may be the best and most truthful answer. Change is the perfect visitor to welcome to the party of *courageous* and *honest* people who are searching for the new way, the better way to deliver value. It's the same guest who always challenges us to be *open-minded and respectful* of the unforeseen impact on others and the unanticipated outcomes we may face. Ultimately, you will have to react and communicate in an *obvious* and *straightforward* manner that will resonate with your family and friends. Commit to simplify and reduce complexity. Your students will respect you even more for demonstrating that you're *mindfully aware* of the impact of change on their lives. Your direct reports will join you in the toughest challenges when you demonstrate your *authentic* self and make it clear that you take *accountability* by the reins with a firm grip, starting with your own role. And you'll build even greater *trust* with your stakeholders when you approach these inflection points of change and challenges in life with the *deliberate and consistent* style that made you feel so emancipated during the good times.

The countless expressions of Steve Jobs' strengths and weaknesses have now been well documented. We can take advantage of these disclosures to adjust our own approach to communication and to life, to be more effective and better than we used to be. Steve shared his own maxim, "You have to trust in something — your gut, destiny, life, karma, whatever. This approach has never let me down, and it has made all the difference in my life." It's time to trust your own ability to embrace the Straight Talk Principles that are about to carry you forward to a whole new level of success and satisfaction!

How to Apply Straight Talk Principle #7:
Be Deliberate and Consistent

This Straight Talk Principle reminds us that trust is essential to long-term success and it can only be developed through *clear and consistent communication.*

- Develop the self-discipline needed to be consistent in what you say and do.
- Make it easy for people to trust you by stating things in a way that can't be misunderstood.
- Deliver bad news and good news the same way — deliberately, consistently and with an example of your personal commitment.
- Keep all your Straight Talk Principles in top condition by exercising them daily.

"Trust is equal parts character and competence... you can look at any leadership failure and it's always a failure of one or the other."

Stephen Covey

What the Research Reveals

A study reported in the publication of the Academy of Management Executives found that two forms of inter-personal trust — trust in a person's *competence* and in a person's *benevolence* — enable effective knowledge creation and sharing. Through interviews with people in 20 organizations including U.S. corporations and government and foreign businesses, the researchers determined that, though conceptually appealing, <u>trust is an elusive concept</u> despite the belief that an organization's <u>success hinges on its ability to create and share knowledge effectively and efficiently</u>.

From their interviews, the group formulated 10 behaviors — "trust builders" — practiced by people who are seen as "trustworthy sources of knowledge."

1. <u>Act with discretion</u>. When someone asks that certain information be kept confidential, doing otherwise violates trust.

2. <u>Be consistent between word and deed</u>. Alignment between talk and action precedes interpersonal trust by allowing people to place credence in what a person says rather than seeking to determine ulterior motives.

3. <u>Ensure frequent and rich communication</u>. More frequent communication increases the amount of

information available to assess abilities, intentions, and behaviors and provides more opportunity to trust in another's competence.

4. <u>Engage in collaborative communication</u>. In an inquiring style of communication, both sides feel free to share and really listen to each other's thoughts and ideas.

5. <u>Ensure that decisions are fair and transparent</u>. Outcomes that are unfavorable for some people are inevitable, but people will still support others if they trust them.

6. <u>Establish and ensure shared vision and language</u>. With common goals and similar jargon and terminology, trust can be increased in informal networks.

7. <u>Hold people accountable for trust</u>. "You get what you reinforce and reward" can be applied to trust as well. You can't measure something so intangible, but it *can* be *recognized*.

8. <u>Create personal connections</u>. People occupy roles that dictate how they "should" act, and these expectations can create an artificial separation that erodes trust.

9. <u>Give away something of value</u>. Giving without expecting something in return is a clear demonstration of trust.

10. <u>Disclose your expertise and limitations</u>. A critical skill is the ability to accurately assess "who knows what." This is particularly difficult when prior interactions are limited or when people don't know much about the problem.

From *Nurturing Interpersonal Trust in Knowledge-Sharing Networks,* by Lisa C. Abrams, Rob Cross, Eric Lesser, and Daniel Z. Levin, published by the Academy of Management Executives.

CHAPTER  8

The Return

"The will to win, the desire to succeed,
the urge to reach your full potential —
these are the keys that will unlock
the door to personal excellence."

Confucius

MY GRANDMOTHER ADELINE isn't the only source of wisdom we can draw upon in our search for greater productivity, greater harmony, and greater success. Straight Talk was advocated 2,500 years ago by Confucius, "Life is really simple, but we insist on making it complicated."

We've come this far together because we must share a common interest — a desire to succeed at even higher levels than we currently enjoy. I hope your desire to reach that full potential will be aided by Grandma's pearls of wisdom and the Straight Talk Principles revealed.

If you want to achieve success in all that you do, don't forget the distinction between wasting your time Smart Talking and really boosting productivity and trust with Straight Talk. You should now be able to recognize some of the most common Smart Talk Traps that seek to trip you up, sap your efficiency, and create confusion. They have the potential to destroy friendships and retard organizational productivity.

The Smart Talk Traps are:
1. Believing that ignorance is bliss.
2. Forgetting that complexity stifles productivity.
3. Thinking that "my way is the only way."
4. Wearing an "empty suit."
5. Denying that pride goes before a fall.
6. Practicing calumny and detraction.
7. Allowing inconsistency to kill credibility and trust.

The antidote for this Smart Talk trash is, of course, the Straight Talk Principles. When followed routinely, they will help you join the ranks of other successful people who soar to greater levels of achievement and satisfaction. They may not be difficult, but they do require daily practice and commitment.

Confucius emphasized the need as well as the challenge of putting good habits into practice: "By three methods we may learn wisdom: first, by reflection, which is noblest; second, by imitation, which is easiest; and third, by experience, which is the most bitter but the most lasting."

It's time to experience the Straight Talk Principles and put them to work immediately:

1. Be aware and stay mindful.
2. Be obvious and keep it simple.
3. Be open-minded and respectful.
4. Be accountable and authentic.
5. Be vulnerable and pocket your pride.
6. Be courageous and honest.
7. Be deliberate and consistent.

I hope this simple, straight forward guide inspires you to begin or to renew a more effective way of communicating and operating. Grandma Adeline was my first Straight Talk teacher and she remains my inspiration to be better than I used to be. I have no doubt you may recognize people in your own life who have pointed you in a positive direction and offered wise counsel that you cherish. I recommend you make it a priority to acknowledge and thank them.

We can now begin our renewal and rejoin the Straight Talkers who enjoy the highest levels of success and harmony. Remember, we all began our lives as Straight Talking children. It's part of our nature, practiced by some and suppressed by others. We may simply have strayed from our origin at the expense of our own well-being. But we can accelerate our return by giving others permission to practice Straight Talk with us.

This may seem obvious, but it's often overlooked in our self-complicated world. Some high-potential conversations and breakthrough moments are just a genie's wish away from the fulfillment of a Straight Talk environment. Grant that wish, and give someone permission to shoot straight with you. By doing so, you invite Straight Talk from others and when they don't feel the need to script, filter, prepare, or position their conversations with you, you're more likely to get the straight scoop. Don't forget to keep your own Straight Talk practice. Keep it real. Keep it simple. Request some feedback. Ask, "How am I doing? Am I shooting straight or have I stepped into those Smart Talk traps?"

After all, we're in this together, so let's make the most out of the great gift we share — communication. We were designed to say what we mean, and we have an obligation to do what we say. Every day, children offer countless examples of Straight Talk in action. As time marches on, we may find ourselves musing about what it would be like to be a kid again. Well, this is one practice — Straight Talk — that doesn't require us to turn back the hands of time! We can renew the practice of our childhood once more and accelerate our path to effective communication and its natural benefits. I believe it's appropriate that we end where we really began, not on *page* one but as we were on *day* one of the life we're living today, Straight Talkers by design.

Welcome back — and please make the most of your return.

Visit www.danveitkus.com for more resources, to contact me directly, and to share your own stories about how your practice of the Straight Talk Principles is improving your life.

—Dan Veitkus
August 2013

Acknowledgments

THIS BOOK would not have been possible without the talent of many hearts and minds contributing to the effort. It would not have been possible or real without the timeless principles taught and lived by Grandma Adeline. I love you.

To my dear wife, Jill and our children for your unwavering support as we share life's journey together.

To Tim Sanders, a true friend, a thoughtful coach and a remarkably gifted author and entrepreneur. Your encouragement made this work possible.

To my editor-for-life and a pearl among her confreres, Veronica Hughes. You're as brilliant as you are fun and creative.

To Michele DeFilippo and Ronda Rawlins and the team at 1106 Design. Thank you for taking a manuscript and creating a masterpiece in design and layout.

A special thanks to a true straight talker, a friend who lives and works with passion and served as a valuable sounding board and contributor to this project, Branden Tsetsilas.

Finally, to the many straight talkers that I've had the pleasure of working with who reinforce my confidence that we can continue to recover from the Smart Talk epidemic and enjoy a more productive and harmonious world together.

About the Author

D AN VEITKUS is a Partner
with RM Nephew and
Associates LLC, a global executive search firm based in Boston,
MA, USA.

RM Nephew is a boutique
firm that specializes in plac-
ing chief executives, functional
officers and leaders, and board
directors. RM Nephew is recognized as a trusted strategic partner to clients, as our profile extends beyond
traditional executive recruiting to actively enroll in the
development of high performance leadership teams in
partnership with boards and chief executives.

Prior to entering the field of executive search and
coaching, Dan served 20 years as a business leader
and executive for private and public companies in the

high-tech sector. His functional expertise includes general management, international operations, sales, marketing, services, learning and development, and entrepreneurial ventures. He has logged millions of miles traveling around the world leading teams, serving customers and building successful business partnerships.

Veitkus' clients value the practical and relevant insights he brings to the executive search and leadership coaching process as a former operating executive, enabling him to provide unique service as a trusted partner and advisor to clients, candidates and executives.

Dan assigns meaningful credit for his success as an entrepreneur and leader to the timeless Straight Talk Principles taught to him by his paternal grandmother, Adeline. These principles have helped him shape and influence positive outcomes throughout his life and he delights in sharing them with those he may be coaching or leading. A perpetual student and an inspiring coach, Dan serves colleagues, clients and audiences around the world as an acting practitioner of the principles outlined in Straight Talk your Way to Success. He has authored a guide that is tested against the reality of living, working, giving and excelling in today's highly competitive, global marketplace.

Visit www.danveitkus.com to contact Dan directly or to solicit his availability to address your team or consult with your organization.

Made in the USA
Lexington, KY
13 June 2014